Leonard Bernstein

Leonard Bernstein

Conductor and Composer

JEAN F. BLASHFIELD

Ferguson Publishing Company
Chicago, Illinois

37777002019578

Photographs ©:AP/Wideworld: 12, 29, 33, 36, 44, 47, 49, 57, 63, 72, 90, 95, 97; Archive: 17, 20, 25, 27, 31, 37, 42, 81, 83, 93; Corbis: 11, 55, 67, 69, 75; Liaison: Tazio Secchiaroli 51, Franco Zeffirelli 84.

An Editorial Directions Book

Library of Congress Cataloging-in-Publication Data

Blashfield, Jean F.
    Leonard Bernstein : conductor and composer / by Jean F. Blashfield.
    p. cm. — (Ferguson's career biographies)
    ISBN 0-89434-337-8
    1. Bernstein, Leonard, 1918– —Juvenile literature. 2. Musicians—United States—Biography—Juvenile literature. [1. Bernstein, Leonard, 1918– . 2. Composers. 3. Musicians.] I. Title. II. Series.
ML3930.B48 B53 2000
780ʹ.92—dc21
[B]   00-037580

CONTENTS

Leonard Bernstein

GROWING INTO MUSIC

ALTHOUGH HE GREW up without music in his home, Leonard Bernstein became America's greatest twentieth-century musician. He had music in his soul, and it came out in many ways. During his life, he composed classical music for orchestras and popular music for Broadway shows, conducted symphony orchestras, introduced television audiences to great works of music, and taught and wrote about music. Leonard Bernstein's influence on music led to a new, worldwide respect for American musicians.

Childhood Years

Bernstein's parents were immigrants from Russia. In 1908, while he was still a teenager, Samuel Joseph Bernstein came to the United States. After working briefly in New York City, he moved to Boston. There, he met Jennie Resnick, also an immigrant from Russia, and the two were married.

Leonard, their first child, was born in Lawrence, Massachusetts, on August 25, 1918. He was given the name Louis, although he was never called that. At sixteen, young Bernstein legally changed his name to Leonard.

Leonard's father was president of Samuel J. Bernstein Hair Company of Boston, which sold supplies to beauty shops. As a young man, Sam Bernstein had worked in a barbershop in Hartford, Connecticut. He hoped that someday his son, Leonard, would join him in the business and eventually succeed him as president.

Leonard and his sister Shirley, who was five years younger, were especially fond of each other. From childhood, they spoke a private language that they called Rybernian. Years later, Leonard dedicated one of the pieces in a composition called *Seven Anniversaries* to his sister. Shirley played an impor-

Leonard Bernstein's parents embraced him after his first concert as conductor of the New York Philharmonic Orchestra.

tant role in Bernstein's life—she was his companion, critic, piano partner, and admirer.

From earliest childhood, Lenny, as he was called throughout his life, demonstrated his intelligence in school. He received excellent grades in public school without working very hard. When Leonard entered junior high school, his father Sam moved the family so that his son could attend Boston Latin School, a famous—and very demanding—public school. The

Lenny with his sister, Shirley, in 1951. The two siblings were extremely close throughout their lives.

schoolwork was so difficult that two thirds of the students were expected to fail and be sent back to regular public schools. Lenny, however, had no trouble succeeding there.

There was no music in the Bernstein home, except for an occasional radio program. Radio was a new invention in those days, and it was hard to get good reception—even with radios so large that they took up part of the living room. Leonard did not really discover music until he was ten years old, when his father's younger sister, Clara, moved to New York City and left her piano with the Bernstein family.

Leonard later said, "From that day to this, it has been very hard to remove me from my keyboard. That's where I suddenly felt at the center of a universe I could control, or at least be at the center of. . . . I was safe at the piano."

Father versus Son

Although he had had no music lessons, Lenny began to create the chords and harmonies that came naturally to him. At age twelve, he began lessons at the New England Conservatory of Music. The lessons were expensive, and Sam Bernstein began to panic at the thought that his son was serious about music.

The only Jewish musicians that Bernstein's parents had known in their childhood in the Ukraine were the wandering musicians called *klezmers*. Many people looked down on these people, and Sam was appalled at the idea that his son would become like them. He was afraid Leonard would end up poor, playing piano in a cocktail lounge somewhere.

Music was the subject of an argument between father and son that lasted for many years—but Sam had mixed feelings about Lenny's serious interest in music. Although he would often urge his son to go into the beauty-supply business with him, Sam bought Lenny a new piano and took him to his first professional concert, performed by the Boston Pops Orchestra. Leonard's mother, Jennie, did not argue with her husband but she quietly supported whatever decisions her son made.

Despite his concerns, Sam was proud of his son's ability. During the early 1930s, when Sam's success in business allowed the family to take vacation cruises, he arranged for Leonard to play for the other passengers on board. He also sponsored a series of thirteen radio programs that featured his teenaged son at the piano.

Days at Harvard

In the fall of 1935, Leonard Bernstein entered Harvard University in Cambridge, Massachusetts, as a music major. While studying there, he became known as a genius piano player who could quickly create jazz versions of classical musical compositions without any preparation. His friend, David Diamond, later said of Lenny's talents, "Lenny in the thirties was unbelievable. There was immense joy in his music-making."

Bernstein also wrote reviews of musical performances for a college magazine, *The Harvard Advocate,* and a professional journal, *Modern Music.*

After he reviewed a new work by composer William Schuman, Bernstein and Schuman became friends. "One simply had an innate feeling that here was a person of absolutely extraordinary ability and that whatever he wanted to accomplish he would," recalled Schuman.

The summer after his sophomore year in college, Lenny worked as the music counselor at a camp in the Berkshire Mountains. The campers were going to perform Gilbert and Sullivan's *The Pirates of Penzance,* and the management hired Adolph Green to help Bernstein. The two young men became friends and later created Broadway musicals together.

Lenny's senior honors paper was titled "The Absorption of Race Elements into American Music." In his paper, Bernstein argued that jazz, which grew out of African-American culture, was the most important American musical phenomenon in the twentieth century.

During this time period, most people regarded jazz as an unimportant, low form of music. Bernstein discussed the influence of jazz in George Gershwin's opera *Porgy and Bess* and the composer's famed piano piece "Rhapsody in Blue." Many people regard George Gershwin as the greatest American-born composer of the twentieth century. Years later, Bernstein would often be called "another Gershwin."

More Musical Training

Bernstein earned his bachelor's degree in 1939. The question was, what to do next? Most American musicians felt inferior to Europeans as far as great classical music was concerned. Most European masters tried to keep it that way, too. They felt that the United States was too young a country and did not have a long-enough musical tradition to create great

As a young man, Bernstein was drawn to the idea of conducting as well as composing.

musicians. Lenny had no urge to study in Europe, however. It was also clear that Europe was about to become involved in a war.

Instead, Leonard decided to attend Curtis Institute of Music in Philadelphia, Pennsylvania. Dimitri Mitropoulos, the Greek-born conductor of the Minneapolis Symphony Orchestra, had suggested that Bernstein try conducting. Lenny had never considered that before. He always thought he would become a concert pianist, which is what his mother had encouraged him to do. At Curtis Institute, he could study both subjects.

For two years, Bernstein concentrated on learning to conduct, studying with the great German-born conductor Fritz Reiner. He also continued to study piano, under Isabella Afanasiovna Vengerova.

While at Curtis, Bernstein conducted a full orchestra for the first time—the student orchestra that Reiner normally himself conducted. The novice found the experience exhilarating, even though he knew he was "just horrible."

Bernstein was the only college graduate in the student body. The other students had studied nothing but music all their lives. Bernstein later recalled that he "was not a smash hit with the student body. As you can imagine, they regarded me as a Harvard smart aleck, an intellectual big shot, a snob, and a show-off." Randall Thompson, the new director of Curtis, was also a Harvard man. He had been hired specifically to change the attitude that Bernstein described. Thompson worked to change Curtis from a music conservatory to a full-fledged college.

While working under Randall Thompson, Lenny continued to broaden his musical education. He learned to orchestrate music. Orchestration is the arrangement of the notes to be played by an orchestra, which may consist of 2, 12, or 100 instruments. To orchestrate music, the arranger must know the sounds and capabilities of every musical instrument—from the kettledrum to the oboe, the violin to the cello and bass viol. Bernstein would rely on his orchestration skills for the rest of his life.

During his years at Harvard, Lenny had spent a lot of time with the Boston Symphony Orchestra. The orchestra's longtime conductor, Serge Koussevitzky, had become his friend and mentor. Koussevitzky founded the Berkshire Music Center at Tanglewood in Lenox, Massachusetts, where the Boston Symphony held its summer concerts.

Serge Koussevitzky, conductor of the Boston Symphony Orchestra, was Bernstein's friend and mentor.

Tanglewood opened in the summer of 1940, while Bernstein was studying at Curtis Institute. He spent that summer studying with Koussevitzky. On July 11, 1940, Leonard Bernstein conducted the Boston Pops student orchestra in an open-air concert. It was his first experience conducting a professional orchestra. At age twenty-one, he was conducting the first orchestra that he had ever heard, seven years earlier with his father.

In the spring of 1941, Bernstein graduated from Curtis as a member of its first class of conducting students. He went to Tanglewood for a second summer of study with Koussevitzky. Then, it was time to starting thinking about a career.

Bernstein had many talents and the determination to succeed at whatever he did—whether composing a children's song, conducting a symphony, or teaching young people about music. He knew he couldn't follow all of his ambitions at the same time, however. He believed he had to make a choice as to which direction he wanted to take or life itself would make the choice for him.

In the end, however, Bernstein never had to make a choice. He did everything.

CHOOSING A DIRECTION

BERNSTEIN ONCE TOLD an interviewer, "When you're conducting you itch to compose, and when you're composing you itch to conduct." After finishing school, Bernstein couldn't scratch either "itch" right away. First, he had to fight a war.

Lenny grew up with left-wing, or radical, political convictions, which he held throughout his life. During his college years, he spoke against joining the forthcoming war against Hitler's Germany—a position he shared with the Communist Soviet Union. When Germany invaded the Soviet Union, however, Bernstein changed his mind.

In 1941, war was already underway in Europe. The United States was yet involved in what would become World War II, but the U.S. Army was gearing up for action. Leonard reported to the draft board. He was turned down for military service, however, because of the asthma he had suffered since childhood. So, instead, Bernstein began to pursue his musical career.

Slow Start in Boston

Leonard Bernstein hoped that he would be able to move directly into a position with a good orchestra. After all, he had been taught by two of the greatest conductors—Fritz Reiner and Serge Koussevitzky.

But that wasn't to be. In the autumn and winter of 1941, Leonard couldn't even find a job. Sam Bernstein continued to hope that his son would join him in the beauty-supply business and give up the absurd idea of making a living in music. Instead, Lenny took small musical jobs around Boston. After Leonard graduated from Curtis, his father had rented a studio for him and bought him a piano. The young musician advertised that he was available to give piano lessons, although very few students arrived.

Leonard gave a few recitals and planned musical programs for some of Boston's museums. He even conducted rehearsals for the Boston Symphony Orchestra. During this time, he also worked again with his old friend, songwriter Adolph Green. The two teamed up with Green's partner, Betty Comden,

Adolph Green and Betty Comden wrote a number of well-known musicals, and Bernstein worked with them many times.

and actress/singer Judy Holliday on a musical called *My Dear Public.* This was Bernstein's first musical—although the friends would work together again many times creating some of the twentieth century's most popular works for United States musical theater.

Lenny was caught in a predicament that kept him from obtaining good work that winter. The American Federation of Musicians controlled most of the good jobs, and he was not a member of that union.

Bernstein wanted to work with the Boston Symphony Orchestra. The orchestra's board of directors refused to let its members join the union. So, if Lenny joined the union, he might be able to get jobs, but he wouldn't be able to work with the Boston Symphony. If he worked with the Boston Symphony, he would later have trouble getting a union card and other work.

In 1942, Koussevitzky took Bernstein on as his assistant during the Tanglewood summer season. Leonard conducted a number of concerts performed by the student orchestra. After that, however, he gave up on Boston and its orchestra and moved to New York City.

Conducting at Tanglewood. Bernstein spent many summers at the Berkshire Music Center.

Success and Failure

Bernstein went to New York City in the fall of 1942, determined to start making a real living in music. A friend found him a job editing jazz music for Harms Publishing Company. Bernstein worked there under the name of Lenny Amber. "Amber" is the translation of the name *Bernstein*. Harms published the first composition that Lenny had written since he graduated from Curtis—a clarinet sonata. Even as he edited other people's music and wrote his own, conducting was never really out of his mind.

That winter, Lenny completed his first large work, the symphony he called *Jeremiah*. He had been working on it for several years. He entered it in a contest for which the main judge was his friend Serge Koussevitzky. The tradition-minded conductor did not like the jazz flavor of the piece, however, and did not award Bernstein the prize. Koussevitzky believed that Lenny's use of jazz would jeopardize his chances of ever conducting a respectable orchestra.

The next summer, Tanglewood did not open because there was a wartime prohibition on the use of gasoline for travel. Lenny couldn't go there to teach, as he had planned, and was beginning to feel useless, as if he didn't have any place in the music world.

At the piano. Bernstein spent countless hours working on new compositions.

Lucky Breaks

In August 1943, Bernstein's luck changed. Artur Rodzinski, the Croatian-born conductor who had just been named musical director of the New York Philharmonic, offered Bernstein a position as his assistant. Beaming with joy, Leonard accepted. He was even given a room to live in at Carnegie Hall, the grand old concert hall in New York City where the orchestra played.

The orchestra board and the public were not as enthusiastic as Lenny was about his new job. Bernstein was American-born, so did not have the same appeal that a European-born musician would have had. He was also Jewish, and at that time there were some people who were prejudiced against people of Jewish heritage and religion. He was also very young—only twenty-five—and some thought he was too inexperienced for the job.

Most assistant conductors never get to actually conduct the orchestra in public. Instead, they may lead rehearsals, preparing the orchestra before the conductor comes in to put on the finishing touches. Bernstein would also conduct when Rodzinski wanted to walk around and hear the music from different parts of the auditorium.

When Artur Rodzinski was named musical director of the New York Philharmonic, he offered Bernstein a position as his assistant.

Lenny was in his new position only a few weeks, however, when two almost miraculous things happened—only one day apart.

On November 13, soprano Jennie Tourel, a friend of Bernstein, made her recital debut at Town Hall in New York City. Bernstein accompanied her in a performance of his song collection called *I Hate Music: A Cycle of Five Kid Songs for Soprano and Piano*. It was the first performance of a Bernstein composition by a professional musician, based on an idea given to Bernstein by his friend Edys Merrill. The soprano plays a ten-year-old girl who sings, "Music is a lot of folk; / In a big dark hall / Where they really don't want to be at all; / . . . But I like to sing." The audience loved Bernstein's amusing and irreverent songs.

Lenny had barely gone to sleep after an all-night celebration when his phone rang. The orchestra's assistant manager was calling to tell him that the guest conductor, Bruno Walter, was ill and would not be able to conduct that day. Rodzinski was snowed in and could not get to the performance either. Bernstein would have to conduct—and there was no time for a rehearsal with the orchestra. That afternoon's concert was to be broadcast live to a nationwide radio audience.

Bernstein accompanied his friend Jennie Tourel on piano when she made her singing debut at Town Hall in New York City.

A Dazzling Debut

Fortunately, the young conductor had done his homework well. He had thoroughly studied the scores and sat through many rehearsals of the various pieces. Walter, even though he was running a fever and felt terrible, asked Bernstein to come to his hotel room. He went over the musical program with Bernstein, explaining to him what the orchestra would need and expect.

On November 14, 1943, Bernstein stepped onto the stage of Carnegie Hall. He later described the performance that night: "It's legendary now, that debut. The audience was out of its head. I remember the pain, at the beginning, of Bruno Zirato [the manager] going on stage to make the announcement about the change of conductors. The groan that went up from the audience! After all, this utterly unknown conductor coming on. I remember standing there and trembling and feeling already rejected by this audience."

He explained that as he played the opening three chords of the first piece, "I knew that everything was going to be all right. Ah, those three chords were so glorious! The orchestra was really with me, giving me everything they had, all their attention."

Although he later claimed that "from the time of my entrance until the time of my last exit I remember nothing," he did remember his father's reaction to the concert. Lenny described Sam Bernstein's response as "baffled. He couldn't understand what happened because he had been so against my being a musician all those years. . . . Here was my father standing there absolutely dazzled, bewildered, stupefied because he had seen thousands of people on their feet screaming and cheering for his little Lenny."

Cheers came, too, from the music reviewer for *the New York Times*. The next morning, Bernstein's debut was described in glowing terms on the front page of the newspaper. "Young Aide Leads Philharmonic, Steps In When Bruno Walter Is Ill," read the headline. The article read, "Enthusiastic applause greeted the performance of the youthful musician, who went through the ordeal with no signs of stress or nervousness."

One editorial read, "Mr. Bernstein had to have something approaching genius to make full use of his opportunity." The concert was a great triumph for the young man. Suddenly, the name Leonard Bernstein was known all over the world—and the

The young genius. Bernstein was only twenty-five years old when he conducted the New York Philharmonic for the first time.

course of musical conducting in America changed forever.

Until this time, Europeans had always conducted large orchestras in the United States. Most Americans assumed that good musicianship could come only from European education and experience. Leonard Bernstein would eventually challenge—and change—that attitude.

Bruno Walter conducting at a rehearsal. Walter's illness one night led to an important opportunity for Bernstein.

Making Choices

Some of Leonard's mentors, including Rodzinski, thought that the young man should stay in his position as assistant conductor to continue to learn. Bernstein was enjoying the acclaim, however. He accepted almost every invitation to appear as a guest conductor for other orchestras—even though he had a contract with the New York Philharmonic. His relationship with Rodzinski began to sour.

Bernstein was finally released from his contract as the New York Philharmonic's assistant conductor and was allowed to appear as guest conductor, both with the Philharmonic and other orchestras. He drew large, enthusiastic audiences wherever he appeared.

Leonard was still torn about what type of work he should be doing. He loved the public life of the conductor. He got a thrill out of conducting a large orchestra to perform a musical composition just the way that he heard it in his head—but he also wanted to be creating those compositions, for classical orchestras and for Broadway shows.

He wrote, "It is impossible for me to make an exclusive choice among the various activities of conducting, symphonic composition, writing for the theater, and playing the piano. What seems right for me at any given moment is what I must do."

During this busy period, Helen Croates was helping Leonard organize his exciting new life. She had been his piano teacher when he was a teenager and had soon recognized young Lenny's talent. Helen became his secretary and personal assistant as Leonard now moved into his busy, new life as a renowned professional musician.

BERNSTEIN THE CONDUCTOR

LEONARD BERNSTEIN did not grow up dreaming about becoming a conductor. He made that decision when he was in college. In his senior year, Lenny composed some music for a theatrical production of the ancient play *The Birds* by Aristophanes. On the night the play was performed, he led the small orchestra—the first time he had ever conducted a group of musicians. It was clear then that he had the talent to be a great conductor.

A conductor does more than just stand in front of the musicians and mark a rhythm.

Bernstein was intrigued by Dimitri Mitropoulos, conductor of the Minneapolis Symphony.

Almost anyone can do that. A conductor must understand the music, peer into the composer's mind, and bring out the best in the musicians and the music. A great conductor contributes as much as the composer did.

Training and Inspiration

Bernstein's decision to become a conductor was also greatly influenced by several important teachers. During his sophomore year at Harvard, he met Dimitri Mitropoulos, the conductor of the Minneapolis Symphony. Bernstein described the Greek-born conductor as "a magician, a wild man," and became fascinated with the person and his work.

Bernstein studied conducting under Fritz Reiner at the Curtis Institute of Music in Philadelphia, Pennsylvania. Before he could enroll in the class, Lenny had to audition. The famous conductor put a musical score (the sheets of written music) in front of the young man. Reiner then asked him to identify the work and play it.

Lenny sounded out the melody in his head and—by sheer luck—it was a tune he had learned in grade school. He knew that the tune was based on a work by the German composer Johannes Brahms. Bern-

Fritz Reiner taught conducting classes to Bernstein at the Curtis Institute of Music in Philadelphia.

stein immediately identified the work for Reiner, sat at the piano, and played it. Lenny was accepted into the conducting class.

Reiner taught Bernstein that, as conductor, he must know every note in a piece of music. If he didn't, he shouldn't conduct it. Lenny later described Reiner as "an intellectual conductor who demanded certain standards of knowledge that were absolutely basic, minimal—and these minimal standards were maximal. . . ."

Reiner would stop a student during a conducting class and demand that the student—without looking at the score—tell him exactly what a particular instrument should be doing at that time. To answer correctly, the student had to have a vision of the whole score in his head—something not many students could do. Bernstein had a talent for it.

Leonard described Serge Koussevitzky, who he studied with at Tanglewood, as having taught him "the essence of the music and the spirit of the music." Bernstein came to regard the Russian conductor as another father.

Koussevitzky described a conductor as a magician who must "unlock the secrets of the composer." Bernstein always believed that the conductor's most important function is to teach. He tried to make his musicians understand what he himself felt about a particular piece of music and how they could express that feeling.

Finding His Place

After the acclaimed 1943 performance of the New York Philharmonic, invitations for Leonard to appear as guest conductor poured in from all over the nation. The following January, Bernstein went to the Pittsburgh Symphony to conduct the world premier of his own *Jeremiah* symphony for Fritz Reiner, featuring Jennie Tourel as the soloist. Koussevitzky then asked him to conduct *Jeremiah* with the Boston Symphony.

Within months, Bernstein was made conductor of the New York City Symphony. This orchestra was not as illustrious as the New York Philharmonic, where Leonard had been the assistant conductor under Rodzinsky—but Bernstein was now a full conductor. He now had the opportunity to select the music his orchestra would play and demonstrate that he was capable of serving as the music director of a major orchestra.

With talent and incredible energy, Bernstein had his own special style while conducting.

Starting a Family

In 1945, Bernstein was presented with another opportunity. He met Felicia Montealegre. The beautiful Chilean-born woman had studied with pianist Claudio Arrau, hoping to be a concert pianist. She eventually gave up music to become an actress on stage and television. After a concert he had given with Bernstein, Arrau hosted a dinner party, where he introduced Leonard and Felicia. Legend holds that the two fell in love at first sight.

Leonard and Felicia were engaged in 1947. On September 9, 1951, they were married at the Bernstein family's synagogue in Boston. Bernstein wore a white suit that had belonged to Serge Koussevitzky, who had died only a few months earlier. The couple later gave their son, Alexander, the middle name of Serge. Their first child was a daughter named Jamie; their third child was named Nina.

Bernstein enjoyed being at home with his family. His daughter Jamie later wrote, "He was really relaxed around us. He liked to get down on the floor and play silly games and let us walk on his back, which was supposed to be therapeutic. He was fun to have around."

Bernstein was greeted by his family and by David Kiser, president of the New York Philharmonic, when he returned from a Latin American tour.

Jamie also watched her father constantly shift the direction of what he wanted to be doing. "There was plenty of trauma in the creative process, both for my father and for those living around him," she wrote. "What was really tough for him was going back and forth between being a conductor—and being very gregarious—and coming home from the road, switching gears, and becoming an introverted, contemplative composer."

Another Milestone

In 1953, Bernstein was faced with a daunting challenge. He had only six days to prepare to conduct the opera *Medea,* which was to open the La Scala opera season, in Milan, Italy. He would be the first American ever to conduct at that world-renowned opera house.

Leonard had been given this opportunity by world-famous soprano Maria Callas, who wanted the talented young man to conduct her. Once again, Bernstein proved his ability to absorb—and to make his own—a work he had not conducted before. The opera-loving and traditional Milanese audience loved him.

Bernstein conducted the world-famous soprano Maria Callas in a performance of Medea *in Milan.*

In those early days, however, not everyone appreciated Leonard Bernstein. For a music class at school, Esa-Pekka Salonen, who later became director of the Los Angeles Philharmonia, attended a Bernstein performance. Salonen's teacher was appalled by Bernstein's performance of Brahms's *First Symphony.*

Salonen, however, felt differently. He later wrote, "There was this piece that we all thought we knew so well, and listening to Bernstein conduct it was like hearing it for the first time. It felt as if he was composing the symphony as he was conducting it."

Moving to the Top

During 1956, the New York music critics began criticizing the way that the New York Philharmonic was being run. They claimed that the programs were too conservative and the performances were becoming dull. The longtime manager of the orchestra was forced to retire.

Dimitri Mitropoulos, who had conducted the New York Philharmonic for two years, issued a statement saying that he and Leonard Bernstein would share the podium for the following year's season. The joint season had just started when it was announced that Bernstein alone would become the New York Philharmonic's music director beginning with the 1958–1959 season.

Mitropoulos was leaving the Philharmonic to take over as the conductor of the Metropolitan Opera. He collapsed during a rehearsal in November 1960, however, and died several days later. A man Bernstein regarded as a "musical father" was gone.

One of the first things that Bernstein did in his new position as music director was make a commitment that, in each of the concerts he conducted, at least one piece of music would be an American composition. In this way, he hoped to gain respectability for American composers. They would no longer be regarded as inferior to Europeans.

The musicians of the New York Philharmonic were among the best in the world. They had worked with the best European-trained conductors and weren't easy to impress. Years before Bernstein arrived, one musician had referred to the group as "Murder, Inc." The forty-year-old Lenny impressed these musicians, however—with his feeling for and knowledge of music and his willingness to treat them with respect, as musicians in their own right.

Lenny's Orchestra

During his eleven years as conductor of the New York Philharmonic, Bernstein turned a good, somewhat uneven orchestra, with falling audience attendance, into one of the world's greatest. Since the orchestra's founding in 1842, no other conductor had held the position of conductor for as long as Leonard Bernstein.

As director of the New York Philharmonic, Bernstein produced more than 200 recordings in eleven years. Many of them are still regarded as the best recordings of some works and are now available on compact discs.

Bernstein's most important accomplishment was to establish musical discipline. He turned a group of individually gifted musicians into a harmonic whole, in which all of the musicians worked together to create the conductor's vision.

New York audiences had almost given up on their city's symphony. The new conductor now had to get the audiences to return. To do that, of course, he had to deliver consistently good music—but Bernstein also thought of another way to get the audiences to listen again. He started talking to them during performances. Every Thursday night, Bern-

Bernstein (at podium) with the New York Philharmonic in 1958. During his time as conductor, the orchestra became respected throughout the world.

stein held an open concert, a sort of glorified rehearsal, during which he described to the audiences what was going on in the music and in the orchestra. Soon, these Thursday night concerts became the "in thing to do" in New York City.

Touring

Bernstein worked the orchestra and himself hard, especially on the long tours that he arranged. In the spring of 1958, the orchestra toured Latin American for seven weeks. They played thirty-nine concerts in twelve countries.

Touring was difficult. Jets were not yet making quick journeys between cities, and each move to a new city was difficult and stressful. Yet, when they arrived in each new city, the orchestra members had to be energized and ready to play.

In 1959, at the request of the U.S. State Department, Bernstein took the New York Philharmonic to the Soviet Union. While standing at the podium, before giving the downbeat, Bernstein turned to the Moscow audience of Soviet music lovers and spoke to them about the importance of artistic freedom.

The Soviet officials were not pleased by Bernstein's speech. At this time, the United States and the Soviet Union were at the height of the Cold War, a period during which the two countries were bitter enemies, although they did not conduct open acts of war.

Dmitri Shostakovich, Russia's greatest living composer, attended the final concert in Moscow to hear the Philharmonic play his great *Fifth Symphony*.

An appreciative audience. Bernstein bowed to the Soviet crowd after a performance of the New York Philharmonic in Moscow.

Eyes on the Conductor

To begin a concert, Bernstein would walk onto the stage, usually to a tumult of applause, bow to the audience, step up onto the podium, and raise his baton. Instantly, even the largest audience would become silent.

One of the things Bernstein liked most about conducting was the public attention and the opportunity to be dramatic. Throughout his life, he relished—and even required—the sound of applause.

Bernstein prepared for each concert by bathing and dressing in clean clothing, from the skin out. He always wore the same pair of cuff links, which had once belonged to Koussevitzky. Wearing them was a sort of charm, a superstition—"the only one I have," he said. He would arrive at the concert hall dressed and ready to go, glance briefly at the score, and then walk on stage.

During a performance, Bernstein never thought about the audience. He thought only of the composer and of the musicians in front of him. He once told an interviewer, "I never think that they are there and I am here. Never. The whole joy of conducting for me is that we breathe together. It's like a love experience."

On more than one occasion, Bernstein had been seriously ill before a concert. The moment he walked onto the stage, however, all traces of weakness seemed to leave him. He conducted with all the strength and brilliance that he did when he was healthy—but the moment he walked off the stage, he would collapse.

After a concert, Bernstein—like many other conductors and performers—always needed many hours to wind down from the high energy of the performance. He would usually go out with friends to eat, chat—usually about politics—and play games, often into the small hours of the night.

After he had totally relaxed, his mind would start racing again, getting ready to deal with the next challenge. Often, the challenge would concern his second career—composing music.

In November 1966, at a large press conference, Leonard Bernstein announced that he would be retiring from the New York Philharmonic at the end of the 1968–1969 season. Of course, he was not going to retire completely. That would have been impossible for Bernstein. He just felt it was time to concentrate on some of the other things he enjoyed doing, and did so well.

BERNSTEIN
THE COMPOSER

ALMOST FROM THE TIME he began to play the piano, Leonard Bernstein was composing new pieces. He spent hours at the piano. In only a few months, he wrote his first piano concerto, not even knowing what it was.

At age fourteen, he and his friends put on a hilarious version of Bizet's opera *Carmen,* for which Lenny wrote simplified versions of the music. The boys—with their new beards and breaking voices—played the women's roles, and the girls played the men's parts.

His first serious composition was "Pianoforte Trio, for Violin, Violoncello and Piano," written in 1937, when Leonard was nineteen years old. Within a few months, he publicly performed another of his compositions, "Music for the Dance Nos. 1 & 2, Music for Two Pianos."

Training and Influences

Most young musicians have to be taught music theory, which is the study of the tone patterns that the different notes of the scale can make. Leonard seemed to have a natural understanding of music theory and harmonies. Composer Walter Piston, who taught Bernstein at Harvard, said, "There wasn't much to teach him. He knew most of it by instinct."

Bernstein had already been playing music composed by Aaron Copland for several years when he met the great composer. During Lenny's senior year at Harvard, he was invited to Copland's birthday party and played the composer's music for him on the piano. Copland complimented Bernstein, saying that he wished he could play his own music as well.

That event began a lifelong friendship between the two men. They became musical partners: Cop-

At Aaron Copland's eightieth birthday celebration. Copland (seated) was a lifelong friend and mentor to Bernstein.

land provided advice on Bernstein's compositions, and Bernstein conducted Copland's music whenever possible, increasing its popularity. Bernstein was committed to encouraging American composers. Copland is known for his use of American themes in his music, such as rodeos and folk songs from the Appalachian Mountains.

With Aaron Copland as his mentor, Bernstein felt no need to study music composition at Curtis Institute and Tanglewood. The two friends continued to work together even as Bernstein approached his startling debut as conductor of the New York Philharmonic in November 1943.

Winning the Hearts of the Public

After that debut, Bernstein, who had been broke only a few months before, was suddenly making it big as a conductor, composer, and performer of serious piano works. As he began to receive more and more invitations to appear as guest conductor, his musical compositions began to receive increased attention, too.

It may have been luck that made Leonard Bernstein become famous so quickly, but it was his own strong preparation for his musical career that made him such a success. When his sudden fame struck, Leonard had been writing music for so long that he had many original compositions to offer to the public.

Bernstein's symphony *Jeremiah* was performed in New York City on February 18, 1944. It was his first major composition to gain public attention—not all good. Several renowned critics did not like the work, but the public did.

Despite the fact that *Jeremiah* did not win Koussevitzky's competition in 1942, it won the New York City Music Critics' Circle award as the most distinguished new American orchestral work in 1944. Many years later, Bernstein referred to that early work as "my poor little symphony," but critics liked it.

Exactly two months after the performance of *Jeremiah,* a very different kind of Bernstein composition had its first public performance. Bernstein had become interested in ballet while working with Copland, who had written a number of ballets. When Jerome Robbins, a choreographer (dance designer) asked Bernstein to work with him, Lenny instantly had a musical idea that enthralled Robbins.

The two men put together a 25-minute ballet that featured three sailors who were on leave in New York City. In this light-hearted story, the sailors compete with each other for the attention of the girls they meet until they have to report back to their ship for duty. In April 1944, the Ballet Theater at the Metropolitan Opera House performed their ballet, *Fancy Free,* and Bernstein himself conducted the orchestra. The ballet was a huge, immediate success. It has been popular ever since and has been performed internationally.

On the Town

During this period, Leonard was also working with his friends Adolph Green and Betty Comden on a musical titled *On the Town*. The story seems similar to *Fancy Free*—three sailors on leave in New York City—but the actions and the music are entirely different in the two compositions.

Despite Bernstein's newfound fame, the three artists had trouble finding money to produce *On the Town* until the well-known director George Abbott, who had liked *Fancy Free*, agreed to direct it.

Although Abbott cut a lot of the numbers that the composers liked, he left in the long, symphonic dance passages choreographed by Jerome Robbins. This type of dance passage was new to Broadway musicals.

The show opened on December 28, 1944, and was another immediate success. One of the songs from this show, "New York, New York," has become New York City's theme song.

As Bernstein became more popular, his former teacher, Koussevitzky, was afraid that the young man was harming his chances to be taken seriously. The public was paying more attention to his jazz-based popular songs than to the serious classical

Bernstein with Jerome Robbins (on couch, right) and Betty Comden and Adolph Green (on floor). This group worked together to create On the Town.

music that Koussevitzky knew Bernstein could write and conduct. Both as a composer and as a conductor, however, Leonard Bernstein never separated the two kinds of music.

In many ways, Bernstein is similar to the talented and popular composer George Gershwin. Some classical musicians look down on Gershwin and consider him primarily a songwriter, which they consider inferior to a composer. Some people also consider Bernstein "just a songwriter" because he, too, wrote music that people loved. Bernstein, however, once described Gershwin as "certainly one of the true, authentic geniuses American music has produced."

Wonderful Town and Candide

My Sister Eileen was a very popular stage play during the late 1940s and early 1950s. The play is about the escapades of two sisters who move to New York City. Several composers had tried to turn the play into a musical but without success. In 1952, George Abbott persuaded the team of Bernstein, Comden, and Green to take a crack at it.

Lenny wrote the score for *Wonderful Town* in less than five weeks. He was able to do this because of a habit he shared with most composers—save music that didn't work in one place and use it somewhere else. Bernstein had saved a number of bits, especially jazzy ones, that came to the rescue. The show opened on Broadway on February 25, 1953. The critics especially liked Bernstein's score.

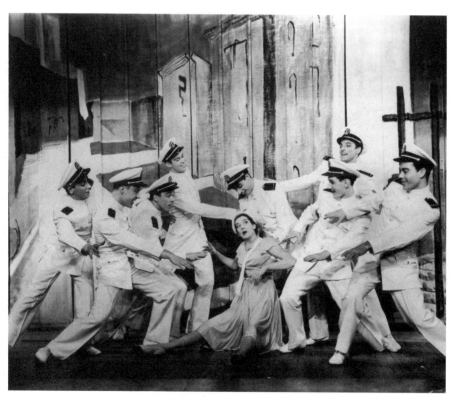

A performance of Wonderful Town. *Bernstein wrote the critically acclaimed score for this musical.*

In 1956, Leonard was invited to become the joint conductor of the New York Philharmonic. Knowing that he would have to be concerned strictly with classical music once he started in that position, he spent part of that year working on another musical, *Candide*. The lyrics, or words, to this humorous opera spoof were written by many famous writers of the time, including Dorothy Parker, playwright Lillian Hellman, and poet Richard Wilbur. The musical opened on December 1, 1956, but it closed after only a few months.

The problem with *Candide* may have been that too many people worked on it. Critics and audiences both thought that it was too fragmented and did not hold together as a single work of art. Bernstein later reworked it—and then reworked it again. His 1973 version of *Candide* is regarded as one of America's greatest musicals.

West Side Story

In January 1949, Jerome Robbins suggested that he and Bernstein create a musical based on Shakespeare's famed star-crossed lovers, Romeo and Juliet. The setting would be the slums of New York City. Instead of Montagues and Capulets, the two fighting communities would be Jews and Catholics.

Bernstein was not sure the idea could work as a musical. Musical-comedy techniques had never been successful used to tell a tragic story.

The two men asked writer Arthur Laurents to create the story, which is called the book. By this time, Bernstein had too many commitments to stay in one place long enough to give the musical the attention it deserved, so the idea was dropped.

Six years later, Bernstein and Laurents turned to the project again—but only briefly. They decided to change the fighting groups to two gangs, one white and one Puerto Rican. Again, they had to drop the project while Bernstein was producing *Candide.*

Finally, in the spring of 1957, as Bernstein was getting more involved with the New York Philharmonic, he knew the time had come. The Romeo and Juliet idea had to be produced or dropped forever.

Bernstein asked Stephen Sondheim to write the lyrics. Robbins worked on the dances. The artists had a difficult time raising the money to present their musical, which they called *West Side Story.* There had never been a violent musical before, and this one ended with the hero lying dead on the stage. They finally did find some brave supporters who came up with the money, however. The new and daring show opened in Washington, D.C., on August 20, 1957.

The musical was a huge success—such a success that some critics thought Bernstein should be ashamed that he accepted the position of conductor of the New York Philharmonic and was going "strictly classical."

Even today, musicians and historians consider *Candide* and *West Side Story* among America's top ten musicals.

Conducting West Side Story *in 1960. The musical was a huge success in spite of its tragic ending.*

Hollywood

Bernstein was enchanted by Hollywood. He even took a screen test to play the role of Russian composer Tchaikovsky in a movie. He never did appear as an actor in a Hollywood film—but he did make it to Hollywood. His score for the film *On the Waterfront,* which made Marlon Brando a star, is regarded as one of the greatest film scores ever and is often played in a symphonic version.

At first, Bernstein had turned down the commission to write the sound track. When he saw an early print of the film, however, he went to work. Bernstein felt that the story was connected to political activities in the United States at that time. In the film, the character played by Marlon Brando stands up to the mob that is controlling the waterfront. During that period in history, individuals were standing up to Joe McCarthy, a senator who was making unproved accusations about their disloyalty to the United States and destroying their careers and lives.

Two Bernstein musicals were turned into Hollywood blockbuster movies. Both were awarded four stars by the critics. In 1949, *On the Town* starred Gene Kelly and Frank Sinatra. When *West Side Story* was released in 1961, it earned ten Academy Awards.

Bernstein and the President

In 1960, Bernstein wrote a Fanfare that was played at John F. Kennedy's inauguration as the thirty-fifth president. The Kennedys later invited him to visit the White House. In 1968, Leonard publicly supported the presidential candidacy of John's brother, Robert Kennedy.

Some years after the assassination of President Kennedy in 1963, Jacqueline Kennedy asked Bernstein to become the director of the new John F. Kennedy Center for the Performing Arts in Washington, D.C. Because it was more of an administrative position than a musical one, however, he did not accept.

In 1968, the president's widow asked Bernstein to compose a piece for the opening of the Opera House in Kennedy Center. For this very special occasion, Bernstein created a theatrical version of the Catholic Mass, with singers, dancers, and actors. Alvin Ailey created the choreography.

To help him finish the work, which was running late, Bernstein asked Stephen Schwartz to help create the text. Schwartz had written the text for the religious musical *Godspell*, which had been a smash success on Broadway.

Bernstein and his family with Jacqueline Kennedy (second from left). The conductor was a supporter and friend of the Kennedy clan.

The composition was performed on September 8, 1971. It ran long, and despite arguments from almost everyone, Bernstein was unwilling to cut anything. The audience, too, found it too long. Although this large and ambitious work was not an immediate triumph, *Mass, A Theater Piece for Singers, Players, and Dancers* has since become very popular.

A Legacy of Invention

Bernstein was not happy with what was happening to classical music in the second half of the twentieth century. He wrote, "Pop music seems to be the only area where there is to be found unabashed vitality, the fun of invention, the feeling of fresh air."

Some critics thought that he should be writing twelve-tone music, a type of music that does not rely on the rules of harmony found in traditional music. In the mid-twentieth century, many composers were creating this type of twelve-tone, or atonal, music. When Bernstein did try to write in this form—in his one full-length opera *A Quiet Place,* produced in 1983—the trend toward twelve-tone music was already ending. The opera was not well received. Although Bernstein always hoped to write the "Great American Opera," he never did.

Throughout his life, Bernstein continued to write many varieties of music—from the pep song called "Get Hep!" for Michigan State College to *The Dybbuk,* another ballet for Jerome Robbins, performed by the New York City Ballet in the spring of 1974. He also wrote works for the piano and for full orchestra. These are still performed as are his two symphonies, *Jeremiah* and *Age of Anxiety.*

BERNSTEIN
THE TEACHER

THE OPENING SENTENCE of *The Joy of Music*, which Bernstein wrote in 1959, reads: "Ever since I can remember I have talked about music, with friends, colleagues, teachers, students, and just plain, simple citizens." And as long as he lived, Bernstein never stopped talking. He was a musician, a conductor, a composer, a writer—but through it all, he was a teacher.

"He was always teaching, a compulsive teacher," wrote Bernstein's daughter Jamie. "His way of saying hello was to share information. So we were always getting it. At your peril you asked him a question."

The Omnibus Series

Leonard's father was the son of a rabbi, and like his father, he turned every situation into an opportunity for teaching. Through the medium of television, Bernstein was able to teach larger numbers of people than any musician has before or since.

In the 1950s, during the early days of television, Leonard taught the viewing audience about classical music on a Sunday afternoon program called *Omnibus*. The program was dedicated to bringing the arts to the general public. Bernstein's first appearance on *Omnibus* was live on Sunday, November 14, 1954. This was exactly eleven years from the day that he debuted as conductor of the New York Philharmonic.

On that first program, he discussed the structure of Ludwig von Beethoven's *Symphony No. 5*. To help the television audience understand what he was talking about, Bernstein arranged to have the famous opening notes of the score painted on the floor of the television studio. He stepped from note to note as he talked about them. He also showed the audience some pages from Beethoven's original manuscript, pointing to notes that the composer decided not to include.

In his program on jazz, he said that what intrigued him is that jazz is "unique, a form of expression all its own. I love it also for its humor. It really plays with notes . . . It 'fools around' with notes, so to speak, and has fun with them. It is, therefore, entertainment in the truest sense."

In his *Omnibus* program, "The Art of Conducting," Bernstein answered a question that he had often heard people ask: What role does the conductor play in the orchestra? Surely, all the musicians are experienced enough to keep the beat and play the notes that are written on the score.

"The first real conductor in our sense of the word was [Felix] Mendelssohn," Bernstein explained, "who founded a tradition of conducting based on the concept of precision, as symbolized in the wooden stick we call the baton." Mendelssohn believed that the conductor had to remain exact to the composer's score. Composer Richard Wagner, on the other hand, believed that the conductor must put his own emotion into the piece. Bernstein explained the difference as "elegance" versus "passion."

Bernstein also explained that a great conductor has to be a great musician. "His instrument is one hundred human instruments, each one a thorough musician, each with a will of his own, and he must cause them to play like one instrument with a single will." He described the conductor as a sculptor whose element, instead of marble, is time.

Bernstein presented several other *Omnibus* programs on such topics as American musical comedy, what makes opera "grand," and Johann Sebastian Bach. Even the least musical person in the audience could appreciate and understand the subjects Leonard presented. Seven of his *Omnibus* scripts, with illustrations, are included in his book *The Joy of Music*.

The Young People's Concerts

Since 1924, the New York Philharmonic had been performing Sunday afternoon programs for children. When people saw how successful Leonard Bernstein was in explaining ideas to his young audience, they suggested that the concerts be televised. As a result, more than forty *Young People's Concerts* were broadcast on CBS Television.

The concerts were first telecast on January 18, 1958, live from Carnegie Hall. Bernstein's first subject was "What Does Music Mean?" Eventually, more than forty nations were able to watch these

Bernstein with participants in a Young People's Concerts *taping in 1961. He enjoyed teaching students, both young and old.*

broadcasts. Bernstein later gathered the scripts for some of the programs in a book meant for young readers.

Bernstein did not like using other people's words. When he had to speak before an audience in a hall or on national television, he wanted to use only his own words. He left the visual content of the television programs to others.

When planning the *Young People's Concerts*, he would pick his subject and write a script—and often entirely rewrite it. He would then hand the script to the producer, who would arrange for the illustrations or visual content that were necessary for a television audience. Without something interesting to look at and learn from, the audience might as well be listening to radio.

The telecast of November 2, 1963, was called "A Tribute to Teachers." Bernstein, himself now a teacher, acknowledged his own greatest teacher, Serge Koussevitzky. Bernstein said, "He taught everything through feeling, through instinct and emotion. Even the purely mechanical matter of beating time, of conducting four beats in a bar, became an emotional experience, instead of a mathematical one."

Television brought many of Bernstein's concerts to people around the world.

Bernstein with his daughter Nina. He made efforts to introduce music to his children and others.

Bernstein's daughter Jamie later wrote, "My brother and sister and I gradually came to think that he was writing the young people's concerts to us. When I became obsessed with the Beatles, Beatles music crept into the young people's concerts. He had a home lab. He was always trying stuff out on us."

For fifteen years, Bernstein's *Young People's Concerts* drew large audiences. His friend Schuyler Chapin wrote, "More than any other musician before—or since—Bernstein understood television's potential to unlock the mysteries of music and make the home audiences care as deeply as he did about the glories of its expressive language."

Making Films

Bernstein was able to—and did—take advantage of all the new communication technologies that were being developed. He was recording the sound for his television programs in stereo at a time when few televisions received stereo sound. As a result, the film of these shows is still enjoyable to listen to today.

After he retired from the New York Philharmonic, Bernstein took particular pleasure in filming concerts that were performed in beautiful settings. He believed that listening to the music was only part of the experience of attending a concert. The first of a series of these films, now recorded on videotape, was the great oratorio (a grand, usually religious, composition for solo singers, chorus, and orchestra) called *Requiem* by Giuseppe Verdi. Bernstein recorded on film the performance at St. Paul's Cathedral in London.

As he did with all of his projects and passions, Bernstein became totally involved in the process of filmmaking. Once, while rehearsing the orchestra for a performance to be filmed in Vienna, the curtain on the stage above the orchestra pit had caught fire—but Bernstein was so engrossed in his work, he didn't notice the commotion that was taking place all around him.

Sometimes, when a concert was being filmed, Bernstein would also arrange for the dress rehearsal to be filmed. He would ask that the audience dress up, too. The dress rehearsals often lasted many hours so that the filming technicians were certain that everything would be right. The work was so fascinating to watch that rarely did the audience members get up and leave before it was done. It might be 2 A.M. before the work was finished, but no one seemed to care—just being in the audience watching was a thrill, and an education.

Teaching at Harvard

In 1971, Bernstein was invited to become the Charles Eliot Norton Professor of Poetry at Harvard University. Other famous musicians, including Igor Stravinsky and Aaron Copland, had also held this one-year position. Leonard had attended Harvard University as an undergraduate and was pleased to receive the honor.

His responsibilities in the position included counseling students on campus and delivering a series of lectures. He was so popular with the students, the student newspaper named him "Man of the Year." Bernstein's series of lectures, known as the Norton Lectures, explored musical language and other concepts. He gave each lecture twice—once at the university and once in a studio so that they could be taped for television.

To explain his ideas, Bernstein often played musical examples on the piano and conducted pieces performed by the Boston Symphony Orchestra and the Vienna Philharmonic. The first lecture, in 1973, discussed Copland's *Piano Variations*, a work that had been one of Bernstein's favorite during his days as a Harvard student.

On Education

In 1977, Leonard Bernstein was asked to testify before a government committee that was studying what Americans thought should be taught in schools. His presentation was televised. He said, "Only a society prepared by education can ever be a truly cultured society. Music desperately needs a prepared public, joyfully educated ears. After all, everyone learns to read words . . . to act in school plays, to have some visual appreciation of graphic forms, to understand a poem by Keats or Robert Frost. But almost nobody is taught to read music, to comprehend its basic principles."

Throughout his life, Leonard Bernstein delighted in helping people comprehend those basic principles. Just before his death in 1990, Bernstein created the Bernstein Education Through the Arts (BETA) Fund. This fund is dedicated to the belief that music is not just for the few, but is vital to the well-being of all people. The organization works both in New York City and throughout the nation to assist teachers in bringing music to students. BETA also supports the work of the Leonard Bernstein Center for Education Through the Arts in Nashville, Tennessee.

Perhaps remembering his own early struggles, Bernstein also changed the education opportunities for young conductors. He established a policy of choosing three assistant conductors through an international competition. This opened up more chances for young people to work with the great orchestras. He also created a learning program for young conductors so that they wouldn't have to just wait for the same kind of once-in-a-million chance that Leonard Bernstein had had.

THE GRAND
OLD MAN

EONARD BERNSTEIN skipped middle age. He went from being Lenny to the grand old man in one jump," said fellow conductor André Previn.

The jump occurred around 1969, when Bernstein retired from the position of musical director of the New York Philharmonic. The administrative tasks of being the musical director of the orchestra were taking up more and more of his time, and he wanted to do more composing.

Bernstein remained the orchestra's first Conductor Laureate, meaning that he would be its officially celebrated conductor for the rest of his life. He simply had to agree to conduct the orchestra at least once a year. This situation would give him the best of both worlds: the delight of conducting people he had worked so hard with but none of the busy administrative work.

An ovation at Tanglewood. Even as he grew older, Bernstein brought enthusiasm and creativity to his work.

Leonard did not stop creating when he "retired." People came to him from all over the world with ideas for projects. Having only a limited amount of time and energy, however, he had to pick and choose what he most wanted to do—and find nice ways to turn away all the others. He traveled around the world, conducting, vacationing, composing, writing, teaching, and raising funds for worthwhile causes.

A Man of Deep Emotion

Although he was small in physical stature, this "grand old man" always seemed larger than life. He was ever on the move, so it's hard to believe that this man suffered from bouts of depression—but he had ever since his adolescent years.

Part of his depression came from his inability to do everything at once. If he was composing—a solitary activity—he wanted to be out in the public. If he was conducting or playing music, part of his mind was back in his own studio composing. While being applauded for his Broadway musicals, he was fearful that he would not be remembered for his great classical pieces. In his later years, Bernstein desperately wanted everyone to love him. He hugged everyone he met, turning them into immediate friends.

In the fall of 1976, Felicia and Leonard Bernstein separated, mainly at Leonard's urging. Months later, she became ill with lung cancer, a disease from which she never recovered. After her death the following year, Bernstein was appalled that he had made her last months so difficult, and he never forgave himself.

Bernstein was a fair and generous person, traits that did not change as his international fame grew. Schuyler Chapin tells of the time that Bernstein was planning to record all nine symphonies by Gustav Mahler with the New York Philharmonic. Bruno Walter had just recorded Mahler's First Symphony. Walter was the last conductor alive who had known and worked with Mahler himself. The initial tape of Walter's recording was so good that Chapin sent it to Bernstein. Bernstein listened and instantly declared, "I couldn't bear the thought of trying to record the work now. It's his!"

Some important reviewers made Bernstein a figure of fun during his great conducting days. They ridiculed the grand gestures he made while conducting, and they scoffed at his "lightweight" compositions for the Broadway stage. Today, more than ten years after Bernstein's death, however,

Grand gestures. Some critics made fun of Bernstein's theatrics, but audiences loved his performances.

many artists are still performing, studying, and recording his works.

In a eulogy published in *National Review,* Chapin described Bernstein as: "Exuberant and uninhibited as a composer, conductor, pianist, educator, and public personality, he was arguably the most talented musician this nation ever produced."

Jewish Faith and Loyalty

Leonard's father, Samuel Bernstein, was the son of a rabbi and a devoted Jew who studied the Talmud, the basic books of Judaism, throughout his life. Leonard and Felicia raised their children in the Jewish faith, and when Leonard was home, he helped them study the Hebrew language.

Because of the prejudice against people of Jewish ancestry, Serge Koussevitzky, hoping to make it easier for Bernstein to be accepted as a conductor, suggested that Bernstein change his name to Burns. Young Leonard refused to consider it.

Throughout his life, Bernstein was deeply troubled by how Adolph Hitler had treated the Jews before and during World War II. He enthusiastically supported the Jewish nation of Israel. He conducted numerous important concerts with the national orchestra there—first in 1947 when it was still the Palestine Orchestra, and many times later when it became the Israel Philharmonic.

In 1967, Bernstein conducted a gala music festival in Vienna, Austria. The highlight of the festival was Mahler's *Resurrection Symphony*. The Austrian-Jewish composer Gustav Mahler's music had been banned by Hitler in pre-war Germany and Austria.

Bernstein conducting the Israel Philharmonic Orchestra in 1948. Throughout his life, he supported Jewish efforts in the music world.

Most of the members of the Austrian orchestra had never played his music. Bernstein had to introduce the work to the musicians, almost as if he were giving a *Young People's Concert*. Because Vienna had been strongly anti-Jewish during the Hitler years, Bernstein was uncomfortable about conducting there. He donated his entire fee to Israel.

In the 1970s, a German company wanted to acquire the rights to productions created by Bernstein's company, Amberson. Leonard did not want his work supported by a German firm. "The war is over, Lenny," his friend Schuyler Chapin reminded him.

At Leonard's funeral, his brother Burton said, "He wanted the whole world to love itself into one big happy family and took it as a personal affront when the world refused to comply. He maintained unflinching optimism and religious trust in the ultimate improvability of man, despite all the evidence to the contrary."

Remembrances

In an interview during the 1940s, Bernstein said, "I'm primarily a conductor. It's not easy to grow as a conductor when you're diverting your energies in

At age seventy. Bernstein remained active in his later years and hoped to be remembered as a composer as well as a conductor.

so many other directions." Just before his death, however, he was afraid that he would be remembered as a conductor rather than as a composer, which is how he wanted to be remembered.

During Bernstein's final months, his friends did not know that he had emphysema, a serious lung disease, but they noticed that he was becoming more and more frail. On August 19, 1990, Leonard conducted what was to be his last concert. Fittingly, it was in memory of Serge Koussevitzky and was performed at Tanglewood in Lenox, Massachusetts. Bernstein and his mentor had come full circle together. Leonard Bernstein died at 6:15 P.M., on October 14, 1990, in New York City.

In his short memorial book, *Leonard Bernstein: Notes from a Friend,* Schuyler Chapin wrote that Lenny was "a man who perhaps more than any other single individual in our lifetime brought excitement, dignity, vitality, and world recognition to American artists. He taught me never to be afraid of passion and never to stop exploring the world."

One of Bernstein's most recent biographers, Joan Peyser, wrote, "What Bernstein did above everything else was prove to the world that an American, and one who had not studied abroad, could be not only well trained but also a remarkable and exciting musician."

Perhaps the greatest compliment paid to this remarkable man came from his own father years before. Some time after Leonard had achieved international fame, Sam Bernstein was being chided for having tried to stop his son from pursuing a musical career. He simply replied, "Well, how was I supposed to know that he was Leonard Bernstein!"

TIMELINE

1918 Leonard Bernstein born on August 25 in Lawrence, Massachusetts

1930 Begins piano lessons at the New England Conservatory of Music

1935 Enters Harvard University as a music major

1937 Writes his first serious composition, *Pianoforte Trio*

1939 Graduates with a bachelor's degree in music and continues his education at Curtis Institute of Music in Philadelphia

1940 Conducts the Boston Pops student orchestra in his first experience conducting a professional orchestra

1942 Moves to New York City after graduating from Curtis Institute and begins working for Harms Publishing Company editing jazz music; assists Serge Koussevitzky at Tanglewood

1943 Meets with Artur Rodzinski, the conductor of the New York Philharmonic, and becomes his assistant

1944 His symphony, *Jeremiah*, is played for the first time on February 18; his hit musical, *On the Town*, opens on Broadway on December 28

1947 Conducts first of many concerts with the Israel Philharmonic

1951 Marries Felicia Montealegre in Boston

1953 Becomes the first American ever to conduct at La Scala opera house in Milan, Italy

1954 Appears on *Omnibus*, a television program dedicated to bringing the arts to the public

1957 *West Side Story* opens in Washington D.C. on August 20

1958 Becomes musical director of the New York Philharmonic and holds this position for 11 years; begins his series, Young People's Concerts, on January 18

1961 *West Side Story* made into a film and wins ten Academy Awards

1968 Bernstein composes *Mass, A Theatre Piece for Singers, Players and Dancers* for the opening of the Kennedy Center Opera House in Washington, D.C.

1969 Retires from his position as musical director of the New York Philharmonic

1973 Reworks *Candide*, now regarded as one of America's greatest musicals

1976 Separates from his wife Felicia

1990 Conducts his last concert on August 19, dies on October 14 in New York City

HOW TO
BECOME
A CONDUCTOR

The Job

Musical conductors direct large groups of musicians or singers in the performance of a piece of music. There are various types of conductors, including those who lead symphony orchestras, dance bands, marching bands, and choral groups. They use their hands, a baton, or both to indicate the musical sound variations and timing of a composition. Their chief concern is their interpretation of how a piece of music should be played. They are responsible for rehearsing the orchestra and auditioning musicians for positions in the ensemble.

Conductors must have the complete respect of the musicians they lead. The greatest conductors have a personal charisma that awes both the musician and the listener. Conductors are unique in the modern musical world in that they make no sound themselves yet control the sounds that others make. The orchestra is their instrument. Musical conductors sometimes carry the title of musical director, which implies a wider area of responsibilities, including administrative and managerial duties. Conducting is an enormously complex and demanding occupation to which only the exceptional individual can aspire with the hope of even moderate success. Conductors must have multiple skills and talents. First and foremost, they must be consummate musicians. Not only should they have mastered an instrument, but they also must know music and be able to interpret the score of any composition. They should have an unerring ear and a bearing that commands the respect of the musicians.

Conductors need to be sensitive to the musicians, sympathetic to their problems, and able to inspire them to bring out the very best they have to offer. The conductor must be a psychologist who can deal with the multiplicity of complex and temperamental personalities presented by a large ensemble of musicians and singers. Composers must exude personal charm; orchestras are always raising funds, and the composer is frequently expected to meet with major donors to keep their good will. Finally, and in line with fund-raising, conductors and musical directors are expected to have administrative skills and to understand the business and financial problems that face the orchestra organization.

The conductor's fundamental purpose in leading, regardless of style, is to set the tempo and rhythm of a piece. Conductors must be sure that the orchestra is following their interpretation of the music, and they must resolve any problems that the score poses. Failure to render a composition in a way that is pleasing to the public and the critics is usually blamed on the conductor, although some feel that both the conductor and the musicians are to blame—or that at least it is difficult to tell which one is most at fault.

The quality of a performance is probably most directly related to the conductor's rehearsal techniques. During rehearsals, conductors must diagnose and correct to their satisfaction the musical, interpretive, rhythmic, balance, and intonation problems encountered by the orchestra. They must work with each unit of the orchestra individually and the entire ensemble as a whole; this may include soloist instrumentalists and singers and also a chorus. Some conductors rehearse every detail of a score while others emphasize only certain parts during rehearsal. Some are quiet and restrained at rehearsals; others work to a feverish emotional pitch.

Requirements

High School Formal training in at least one musical instrument is necessary for a future as a conductor. Keyboard instruction is particularly important. In high school, participation in a concert band, jazz ensemble, choir, or orchestra will teach the student about group performance and how the various parts contribute to the whole sound. Some high schools may offer opportunities to conduct school music groups.

Postsecondary It is uncommon for people to start out at a very early point in life to become a musical conductor. Most conductors begin studying music at an early age and, at some later, more mature point of life discover or suspect that they have the qualities to become a conductor. Some conductors become involved at the high school or college level, leading a small group for whom they may also do the arranging and possibly even some composing.

There are some courses specifically in conducting at advanced institutions, and interested students may take courses in composition, arranging, and orchestrating, which provide a good background for conducting. Some opportunities to conduct may arise in the university, and it is sometimes possible for aspiring conductors to study with a faculty member who conducts the school orchestra. There are also conductor training programs and apprenticeship programs, which are announced in the music trade papers.

Conductors must acquire a multiplicity of skills in order to practice their art. These skills may be divided into three parts: technical, performance, and conducting. Technical skill refers to a conductor's ability to control orchestral intonation, balance, and color. Conductors must be advanced at sight reading and transposition in order to cope with orchestral scores. They must acquire a comprehensive knowledge of all orchestral instruments and have mastery of at least one instrument, the piano probably being the most helpful. They must acquire skills in composition and musical analysis, which presumes accomplished skills in counterpoint, harmony, musical structures, and orchestration. Finally, conductors must understand and be able to adapt musical styling.

Exploring
The best way to become familiar with the art of conducting is to study music and the work of the great conduc-

tors. It is not possible to understand conducting beyond the most superficial level without a good background in music. Students should go to as many musical presentations as they can—symphonies, operas, musical theater, and other types of performances—and study the conductors, noting their baton techniques and their arm and body movements. The student must also observe how the orchestra and audience respond to the gesturing of the conductors.

Employers

There are many situations in which conductors may work. Music teachers in schools often take on the work of conducting as a natural extension of their duties. Conservatories and institutions of higher learning frequently have fine orchestras, choruses, and bands that often choose conductors from the faculty.

There are numerous summer festivals that employ conductors, and conductors may also find positions with community orchestras and choruses, local opera companies, and musical theater groups; amateur groups sometimes hire outside conductors, too.

Starting Out

A career in conducting begins with a sound musical education. Working as an instrumentalist in an orchestral group under a good conductor whose technique can be studied is an important step toward conducting.

The piano is an important instrument for the conductors to know, because it will enable them to score and arrange more easily, coach singers (which many conductors do as a sideline), and rehearse the orchestra as assistant conductor. That is not to say, however, that other instrumentalists do not also have a good background for conducting.

With a solid foundation in musical education and some experience with an orchestra, young conductors should seek any way possible to acquire experience conducting. There are many grants and fellowships available, and many summer music festivals advertise for conductors. These situations often present the opportunity to work or study under a famous conductor who has been engaged to oversee or administer a festival. Such experience is invaluable because it provides opportunities to explore various other conducting positions. Such positions may include apprenticeships, jobs with university choirs and orchestras (which may include a faculty position), or opportunities with community orchestras, small opera companies, or amateur groups that seek a professional music director. These experiences might then lead to offers to work as an assistant or associate conductor with a major orchestra or an opera or musical theater company.

Advancement

There is no real hierarchy in an orchestra organization, so one cannot climb to the role of conductor. The most likely path of advancement would be from the positions of assistant or associate conductor or head first violinist—that is, the concertmaster. Conductors generally move from smaller conducting jobs to larger ones. A likely advancement might be from a small community orchestra or youth orchestra (probably a part-time position) to a small city orchestra (full- or part-time), and from there to a larger city orchestra, a mid-sized opera company, or a middle-level television or film company. Such advancement presumes that the conductor has had sufficient recognition and quality reviews to have come to the attention of larger musical groups.

When conductors receive national or international recognition, they must decide which major position they will accept as openings occur. It is unlikely that a major city orchestra would promote someone within the organization when the position of conductor is open. It is more probable that a search committee will conduct an international search to find a "big name" conductor for the post. Conductors can also advance to top-level administrative positions, such as artistic director or executive director.

Work Environment

The working conditions of conductors range as widely as their potential earnings do. The conductors of small musical groups at the community level may rehearse in a member's basement, a community center, a high-school gym, or a church or temple. Performances may be held in some of these places, too. On the other hand, conductors of major orchestras in the larger metropolitan centers usually have ideal working conditions, generally having the same outstanding facilities for rehearsal and performance. Many universities, colleges, and conservatories—even some of the smaller ones—also have state-of-the-art facilities.

Earnings

The range of earnings for conductors is very wide, and varies from one category of conductor to another. For instance, many conductors work only part-time and make small yearly incomes. Conductors of dance bands, for example, may make from $300 to $1,200 per week. Opera and choral-group conductors make as little as $8,000 per year working part-time at the community level. Salaries range to more than $100,000 per year for those with permanent positions with established companies in major cities. The same applies to symphony orchestra conductors who, for instance, make $25,000 to $40,000 per year conducting smaller, regional orchestras, but who might make $500,000 or more a year if they become the resident conductor of an internationally famous orchestra.

Outlook

The operating costs for an orchestra continue to grow every year, and musical organizations are constantly trimming budgets. This situation has affected growth in the orchestra field and, likewise, the number of available conducting jobs. In addition, the overall number of orchestras in the United States has grown very little in the last two decades. The number of orchestras in academia declined slightly, while community, youth, and city orchestras increased slightly in number. The slight growth pattern of orchestra groups will not accommodate the number of people who graduated from music school during that period and are trying to become conductors. The competition for conductor jobs, which is already tight, will become even more fierce in the next decade. Only the most talented people moving into the field will be able to find full-time jobs.

TO LEARN MORE ABOUT CONDUCTORS

Books

Comstock, Ariane Csonka. *The Young Person's Guide to Opera*. Santa Cruz, Calif.: Monarch Media, 1997.

Geras, Adele. *The Random House Book of Opera Stories*. New York: Random House, 1998.

Gilmore, Donald M. *The Fabulous Song*. Brooklyn, N.Y.: Kane/Miller, 1998.

Simon, Charnan. *Seiji Ozawa: Symphony Conductor*. Chicago: Childrens Press, 1992.

Tan, Sheri. *Sieji Ozawa*. Austin, Tex.: Raintree/Steck-Vaughn, 1997.

Websites

American Symphony Orchestra League
http://www.symphony.org
An organization that provides leadership and support to

American orchestras and promotes their efforts to the public

Conductors' Guild, Inc.
http://www.conductorsguild.org/
A group that encourages and promotes the art of conducting

The Joy of Conducting
http://friko3.onet.pl/kr/lennyb/index.html
A site providing information about conductors, workshops, anecdotes, and orchestras

Where to Write
American Federation of Musicians of the United States and Canada
1501 Broadway, Suite 600
New York, NY 10036

American Guild of Musical Artists
1727 Broadway
New York, NY 10019

American Symphony Orchestra League
1156 15th Street, N.W., Suite 805
Washington, DC 20005

Conductors' Guild, Inc.
103 South High Street
Room 6
West Chester, PA 19382

HOW TO
BECOME
A COMPOSER

The Job

Composers create much of the music heard every day on radio and television, in theaters and concert halls, on recordings, and in other mediums of musical presentation. Composers write symphonies, concertos, and operas; scores for theater, television, and cinema; and music for musical theater, recording artists, and commercial advertising. They may combine elements of one style of music with another—for example, classical music with popular music, such as rock, jazz, reggae, folk, and others.

Composers express themselves with music much as writers express themselves with words and painters with lines, shapes, and colors. Composing is hard work. Although composers may be influenced by what they hear, they create original compositions that reflect their own interpretation and use of musical elements. All composers use the same basic musical elements—including harmony, melody, counterpoint, and rhythm—but each composer applies these elements in a unique way. Music schools teach all the elements that go into composition, providing composers with the tools needed for their work. How the composer uses these tools to create music is what distinguishes the individual artist.

A composer who wishes to make a living by writing music should understand the musical marketplace as well as possible. Only a small percentage of music composers can make their living solely by writing music. To make an impact in the competitive marketplace, one must be familiar with its major components:

Performance. Composers usually arrange to have their music performed in one of two ways: They contact musical performers or producers who are most likely to be receptive to their style of composition, or they write for a musical group in which they themselves perform.

Music Publishing. Music publishers seek composers who are talented and whose work they feel it will be profitable to promote. They take a percentage, or cut, of the royalties, but they relieve composers of all of the business and legal details of the profession. Some composers, however, publish their own works.

Copying. A musical composition written for several pieces or voices needs to be copied for each of the various parts. Composers may do this work themselves, but it is an exacting task for which professional copiers may be employed. Many composers take on copying work as a sideline.

Computerization. Computers have become an increasingly important tool for composers. Some composers have set up sophisticated computerized studios in which they compose, score, and play orchestrated pieces. They can also do the copying and recording by computer.

Recording. A good knowledge of the recording industry is important in advancing a composer's career. An unrecognized composer will find it difficult to be represented by a commercial recording company. Today, composers frequently make their own recordings and handle the distribution and promotion, too.

Film and Television. There is a very large demand for original compositions for feature and industrial films, television programs, and videos. The entertainment and commercial industries are in constant need of original scores and thematic music. Students interested in composing for these markets can tap into any number of organizations and associations for more detail on any aspect of musical composition. One organization that provides support and information is Meet the Composer, which has its headquarters in New York City and affiliates throughout the country.

Requirements

High School   There is no specific course of training for a composer. Many composers begin composing at an early age and receive tutoring and training to develop their talent. Musically inclined students should continue their private studies and take advantage of all the musical programs that their high schools offer. Gifted students usually find their way to schools or academies that specialize in music or the arts, where they might be encouraged to create original compositions.

Postsecondary   After high school, music students can continue their education in any of numerous colleges and universities or special music schools or conservatories that offer bachelor's and advanced degrees. The composer's course of study includes courses on music history, music criticism, music theory, harmony, counterpoint, rhythm, melody, and ear training. In most major music schools, courses in composition are offered along with courses in orchestration and arranging. Almost all schools offer courses in voice and the major musical instruments, including keyboard, guitar, and, more recently, synthesizer. Most schools now offer instruction in computerized music techniques, too. A student interested in composing may also benefit from learning at least one foreign language; German, French, and Italian are good choices.

Exploring

Programs offered by local schools, YMCAs, and community centers offer good opportunities to learn about music. People interested in composing will also find it helpful to learn to play a musical instrument, such as the piano, violin, or cello. Attending concerts and recitals and reading about music and musicians and their careers will also provide good background and experience. There are also many videotapes available through schools and libraries that teach young people about music. Young musicians should form or join musical groups and attempt to write music for the groups to perform. There are also many books that provide good reference information on careers in composing.

Employers

Generally, composers are self-employed. They complete their work in their own studios and then try to sell their pieces to music publishers, film and television production companies, or recording companies. Once their work becomes well known, clients (film and television producers, dance companies, or musical theater producers) may commission original pieces from the composers for a particular production. The client would then provide the composer with a story line, setting, time period, mood, and other specifications for the work. The composer must consider all of these elements when creating the musical score.

Occasionally, there are a few "house" composer positions in advertising agencies or studios that make commercials, or at film, television, and video production studios.

Starting Out

While in school, young composers should try to have their work performed at school concerts or by local school or community ensembles. To do this, the composer will also most likely have to copy and score their work and possibly even direct the musicians.

Student film projects provide an excellent opportunity to gain experience at composing and scoring for films. Working in school or local musical theater companies can also be beneficial. Personal connections made while working on these projects may be very helpful once the young composer is out in the professional world. Having a portfolio of work to present will also prove helpful when beginning to pursue a musical career.

Advancement
Moving ahead in the music world happens strictly on an individual basis, based on talent, achievement, and luck. There is no organizational "ladder" to climb. In some record companies, however, a person with music writing ability might move into a producing or A&R (Artists & Repertoire) job and be able to exercise compositional skills in that position.

Composers may progress through their careers by writing music of greater complexity and in more challenging structures. Some composers become well known for their work in a particular form of composition. Others may develop a unique style, with the hope that, one day, their names might be added to the list of the world's great composers.

Work Environment
The physical conditions of a composer's workplace vary according to personal taste and budget. Some work in expensive, state-of-the-art home studios; others in small rooms equipped with only an electric keyboard or a guitar. An aspiring composer may be just as creative in a cramped and cluttered room in a New York City tenement as in a sprawling home in Hollywood, California.

Earnings
A few composers make huge annual incomes; many others make little or no money. Sometimes, a composer may

make a large income for one or two years, and then make nothing for several succeeding years. Although many composers receive royalties on repeat performances of their work, most depend on client commissions to support themselves. The fees for commissions vary widely according to the type of work, and the industry for which the work will be performed. A survey conducted by the organization Meet the Composer in 1992 compiled current examples of typical fees.

In concert music and jazz compositions, commission fees are based on the length of the work. The fees also vary according to the complexity of performance—ranging from piano solo or duo with instrument or voice, trio or quartet, chorus, small or large chamber orchestra, and full orchestra concerto.

Composers for dance works and companies generally receive a similar range of fees. Prices paid for incidental music composed for the theater are based on the size and type of the theater company or play. A regional company may pay in the $3,000 to $8,000 range, an off-Broadway show pays from $3,000 to $6,000, and a Broadway show from $5,000 to $12,000. In musical theater, the composer may receive an advance of up to $10,000, which is deducted from future royalty payments. Each composer negotiates his or her own royalty rate, which is generally computed as a percentage of the box-office receipts.

Opera companies commission works for one-act operas and full-length operas. A small company may pay in the range of $10,000 to $20,000 for a one-act opera and $30,000 to $70,000 for a full-length opera. Larger opera companies pay from $15,000 to $40,000 for a one-act opera, and from $75,000 to $150,000 for a full-length opera.

The music budget for a film ranges from 1 percent to 10 percent of the total production cost. A major studio may pay a composer $50,000 to $200,000 or more for the musical score for a film. An independent or television film producer may pay in the range of $5,000 to $100,000. Documentary films pay in from $2,000 to $20,000.

For a television program or series, a composer may be paid by the episode—from $1,000 to $8,000 each, depending on the length of the episode and whether the company is a network, cable, or independent television company. Composers working for television advertisers generally receive a flat fee of 10 to 20 percent of the budget for the commercial. Payment ranges from $300 for a regional commercial; up to $20,000 or more for a national commercial; and up to $50,000 if the music is to be a musical "logo"—intended to create a unique identity for the company or product advertised.

Outlook

The field of musical composition does not respond to the economic cycles of recession and prosperity. As a result, the employment outlook for composers probably does not change from year to year in the United States. There are no reliable statistics on the number of people who make their living solely from composing, however— although the general consensus is that very few people can sustain themselves through composing alone.

TO LEARN MORE ABOUT COMPOSERS

Books

Bergaamini, Andrea. *Beethoven and the Classical Age.* New York: Barron's Juvenile, 1999.

Preston, Katherine. *Scott Joplin: Composer.* New York: Chelsea House, 1987.

Sabin, Louis. *Ludwig Van Beethoven.* New York: Troll, 1992.

Venezia, Mike. *Aaron Copland.* Danbury, Conn.: Children's Press, 1997.

Venezia, Mike. *George Handel.* Danbury, Conn.: Children's Press, 1997.

Websites

American Federation of Musicians of the United States and Canada

http://www.afm.org

For information about this union of professional musicians

American Society of Composers, Authors, and Publishers (ASCAP)

http://www.ascap.com

A union representing composers, songwriters, lyricists, and music publishers

Broadcast Music, Inc. (BMI)

http://www.bmi.com/

A company that represents and protects the rights of songwriters and other musicians

Where to Write
American Composers Alliance

170 West 74th Street
New York, NY 10023

American Federation of Musicians of the United States and Canada

1501 Broadway, Suite 600
New York, NY 10036

American Women Composers, Inc.

c/o George Washington University
Department of Music
B-144 The Academic Center
Washington, DC 20052

Broadcast Music, Inc. (BMI)

320 West 57th Street
New York, NY 10019

TO LEARN MORE ABOUT LEONARD BERNSTEIN

Books

Hurwitz, Johanna. *Leonard Bernstein: A Passion for Music*. Philadelphia: Jewish Publication Society, 1993.

Venezia, Mike. *Leonard Bernstein*. Danbury, Conn.: Children's Press, 1997.

Websites

Arias and Barcarolles: The Bernstein Pages

http://www.users.globalnet.co.uk/~mcgoni/

Information about Bernstein's life including a chronology and guide to opera and theater works

Leonard Bernstein

http://www.ny.boosey.com/composerpages/bernstein.html

Provides biographical details as well as performance clips

The Leonard Bernstein Collection
http://memory.loc.gov/ammem/lbhtml/lbhome.html
His works compiled by the Library of Congress

The Official Leonard Bernstein Site
http://www.leonardbernstein.com
An comprehensive site that provides information about recording, publications, concerts, and other materials.

Sony Classical Artist: Leonard Bernstein
http://www.sonyclassical.com/artists/bernstein/
A biography and discography provided by Sony

Interesting Places to Visit
Carnegie Hall
57th Street and 7th Avenue
New York, New York 10019
212/ 903-9790

The John F. Kennedy Center for the Performing Arts
2700 F Street, NW
Washington, D.C. 20566
800/444-1324

Lincoln Center for the Performing Arts
65th Street at Broadway
New York, New York 10023
212/875-5370

Tanglewood Music Center
West Street
Lenox, Massachusettes 01240
413/637-1600

INDEX

Page numbers in *italics* indicate illustrations.

ABOUT THE AUTHOR

Jean Blashfield has written about ninety books, most of them for young people. She likes best to write about interesting places, but she loves history and science too. In fact, one of her big advantages as a writer is that she becomes fascinated by just about every subject she investigates. She has created an encyclopedia of aviation and space, written popular books on murderers and house plants, and had a lot of fun creating an early book on the things women have done, called *Hellraisers, Heroines, and Holy Women.*

In Wisconsin, she delighted in finding TSR, Inc., the publishers of the *Dungeons & Dragons* games. At that company, she founded a new department to publish fantasy gamebooks and novels, and helped the company expand into a worldwide enterprise.

Ms. Blashfield lives in Delavan, Wisconsin.